MY MOTHER'S BLACK CHILD

By

NECHOLIA JOHNSON BECK

My Mother's Black Child

All Rights Reserved © 2004 by Helm Publishing

No part of this book may be reproduced, or transmitted in any from or by any means, graphic, electronic, or mechanical, including photocopying, recording, taping, or by any information storage retrieval system, without the permission in writing from the publisher or author.

Helm Publishing

For information address:
Helm Publishing
3923 Seward Ave.
Rockford, IL 61108
815-398-4660
www.publishersdrive.com

ISBN 0-9723011-7-8
Library of Congress Control Number
Printed in the United States of America

To,
Joyce

Best Wishes
Mechelle Johnson Beck
2004

DEDICATION

This book is dedicated to Nathaniel Johnson, and R.C. Pettigrew

SPECIAL DEDICATION

To My Sister, Roberta

**I'd like to thank you for being there for me when Mom died. You were the only one of my sisters demonstrating strength and love during Mom's funeral. I always told you I would never forget your kindness and I never have.
I love you dearly, and thank you so very much.**

ACKNOWLEDGMENTS

I'd like to thank God for giving me the strength to write this book, and I'd like to thank Dianne Helm, my editor and publisher, who believed in me.

I give special thanks to my two children, Cory, Ericka, and their families who gave me a lot of encouragement and support. I love you all dearly. Last of all, I'd like to thank a friend of mine, Paula Lambert, who also supported me.

Chapter 1

In the early 1940's, Willie Johnson Jr., and Reather Cook were married in Gurdon, Arkansas. Reather married Willie mainly to get away to from home. Reather was raised by her grandmother, Paralee Hubbard. Paralee was very strict and considered herself a woman of color, which meant she didn't like dark-skinned people. Paralee was extremely fair-skinned. Reather also had a brother and two sisters.

Her brother Jim was fair-skinned, but Opal and Eva Mae weren't as light-skinned as Jim. Neither was Reather and she always hated that. She wished with all her might that she had been born with Jim's color of skin. Her grandmother would always favor Jim over Opal, Eva Mae, and Reather.

Necholia Johnson Beck

Reather was hurt a lot by that so that was why she decided to marry Willie, anything to get away from home.

But Willie was very dark-skinned and all of his family was the same. Reather couldn't stand being around all those dark-skinned people. Sometimes she would pretend he was light-skinned just the way she wished she was.

Willie had three brothers, Vernon, Jerry and Bill. He also had one sister, Mattie. Willie was raised by his father, Shorty Johnson and stepmother, Rutha. Willie's mother, Hadie and Shorty had divorced when the children were small. After the divorce, Hadie took one brother and the sister to live with her, while Willie and his other two brothers stayed with Shorty and Rutha.

On February 8, 1944, Willie and Reather had their first child. It was a boy and they named him Nathaniel. He was not at all what Reather had hoped for her first baby to look like. He had dark skin and that alone was enough to make Reather doubt her love. Willie, however, was very proud.

Reather didn't have a mother's love for Nathaniel because he was too black for her. She just couldn't accept that! Willie decided to give Nathaniel a nickname. He called the baby Bo. Shorty and Rutha loved Bo dearly and they kept him most of the time. Rutha could see how Reather mistreated Bo, so she would scold Reather, "You should not treat Bo the way you do and someday the Lord will punish you."

My Mother's Black Child

Reather would always reply, "I can't help it! He's too dark, and I didn't want my baby to be dark!"

"How could you say such a thing about your own flesh and blood?" Rutha asked

"One day," Reather answered her, "I'll have a light-skinned baby and then you and Mr. Shorty can have Bo because I don't want him!"

Rutha cried at those words, which sounded so cruel to her, and said, "Whenever that day comes, Shorty and I will take him to raise if Willie wants us to, because you are not the right mother for him."

Reather just strutted off and thought to herself, *I know you will take him. I don't want him.*

Later, Rutha told Willie how Reather had felt about Bo. He got very angry and said he was going to straighten things out with Reather, but Rutha knew in her heart that he could not change Reather's mind.

Willie went home and asked Reather, "Why did you say you didn't want Bo and why did you say he was too dark?"

Reather replied, "Because it is true. I don't want Bo and you and your family can say whatever you want about me!"

Willie was surprised and hurt by the hateful things Reather had said, so he slapped her across the room. "Shut up!" He yelled at her, "Don't you ever say anything like that again!"

Reather cried and said nothing more.

Necholia Johnson Beck

The next day, Bo was crying because he was teething and trying to crawl around the house. He managed to get into Reather's dusting powder. When she saw what he had done, she hit him on his head and it left a lump. She hollered, "Bo, stop crying and stay out of my things. Just look at this mess you made. You look like a fly in buttermilk with your little black self!"

Bo stopped crying when Reather threw him on his bed and shut the door. She thought, *I have just got to find a way to get out of this marriage and motherhood to a baby I don't even want! Oh, how I wish Bo were light like Jim, then everything would be all right.*

That night, Willie came home from work and noticed the lump on Bo's head. "Why has Bo got a lump on his head?" he asked.

Reather replied, "I did it because he is always getting into things he shouldn't."

Willie felt himself getting angry, "Girl are you crazy? You're going to kill this baby and I won't stand for that! You hate black so much until you can't stand your own son. That is very sad."

"You're right," she countered, "I don't like black and one day I'll show you all just how much I don't like black."

Three days later, Willie decided he would have to keep Bo with him as much as possible and not let Reather be alone with him because he didn't know what she might do next. "I'm going over to

My Mother's Black Child

Daddy's and I'm taking Bo with me, so get him ready," Willie told her.

Reather replied, "Ok." She knew exactly why Willie was trying to spend so much time alone with Bo, and that was just fine with her.

After Reather got Bo ready, Willie took him and left. Then she decided to go over to Dorthy's house. Dorthy was Reather's first cousin. They didn't always get along because Dorthy didn't like the way Reather felt about wanting to be lighter skinned. They sat on the porch, drinking Kool-aid when Dorthy asked, "How are you and Willie getting along?"

"Not so good," she answered, "Willie thinks I'm crazy for feeling the way I do about Bo, and now, he spends as much time as he can alone with him."

Dorthy shook her head, "He's absolutely right. You are crazy, and one day you will pay for all the wrong things you've done to that baby!"

"I don't care," Reather retorted, "You're just like those Johnson's, but you'll see, I'll show all of you one day." With that she left and went home.

Reather was already asleep when Willie and Bo returned from his parents, so Willie got Bo ready for bed. Then he went to bed.

For a few months, things went smoothly. Reather started doing housekeeping work for some white people in Gurdon. Now, she had a little money of her own. It made her happy to work because she could buy some pretty new clothes for

Necholia Johnson Beck

herself. She didn't buy anything for Bo except some diapers, and by now, he really didn't need them since he was two-years-old and toilet trained.

One Sunday morning Reather told Willie she wanted Mr. Shorty and Rutha to start keeping Bo because she could not work and take care of him.

Willie sneered, "What you really mean is you don't want Bo because he is too black for you!"

"Yes, and if you don't do it, I'll leave and go to Rockford."

Rockford was a fairly large city in Illinois and it was where Reather's brother Jim and his wife, Vera lived.

Willie looked at Reather. He shook his head sadly as he said, "Ok, I'll ask Daddy. If he says yes, you know if they take him, you'll never be able to get him back."

"That's just fine with me," Reather coldly replied.

Later that evening, Willie went over to his daddy's house and asked if he and Rutha would keep Bo. They both said yes.

Shorty cried, "Reather is crazy, but Bo is my grandson and I don't want him to live with Reather. She could get mad one day and we could find Bo dead somewhere."

Rutha agreed, "Yes, Willie. Bring him over in the morning and we'll be more than glad to keep him."

My Mother's Black Child

The next morning Willie got up for work. He took Bo over to Shorty and Rutha's house. Willie told Bo he was going to stay with Grandpa and Aunty Boo for a while, but daddy would come see him everyday. Being too little to understand why he would be staying with Grandpa and Rutha, Bo said, "Ok."

With a heavy heart, Willie went to work crying and praying to God to watch over Bo and make things right.

One month later, Reather had gotten a job doing housekeeping for this widow white man. He told her that he liked the way she cleaned his house. He asked her if she could come three days a week instead of one day a week from then on. She agreed to that and he informed her that the key would be in the mailbox outside if he wasn't there.

The following week, Reather went over to Mr. H.B.'s house and sure enough, the key was in the mailbox just like he said it would be. Reather unlocked the door and went inside the house. She started to clean the kitchen first and then the living room afterwards, with the bedroom last. When Reather was finished with the last bedroom, all of a sudden Mr. H.B. appeared from out of nowhere, naked as a jaybird! Reather turned and said, "Oh! I didn't know you were here."

He half-smiled and said, "I know you didn't, but that's all right because I planned it that way!" He advanced towards Reather and kissed her, unbuttoning her dress as he did. By that time,

Reather began to like the attention. Mr. H.B. told her she was pretty and had wanted her for a long time. Reather smiled at that. Then he told her to take off her panties, which she did. They made love and the sweat from his body was all over Reather. Reather reveled in the whole experience. She liked the way he made love to her, but she knew Willie or anybody else could never know that this had happened. So she got up and took a bath. When she finished and came back to the room, there was a five-dollar bill lying on the pillow. When she saw the money, Reather knew she had just been used, and started crying. She felt so ashamed.

Reather decided that she would never houseclean for that man again. Willie was there when she arrived home. He asked, "What did you do today?"

Reather got scared right away, and thought, *How did he find out?* She looked at him and asked, "Why?"

"Oh, nothing, I just asked."

Breathing an inward sigh of relief, Reather thought, *Oh, he doesn't know. Thank God.* She casually replied, "I cleaned Mr. H.B.'s house today."

"Did he pay you?"

"Yes, but not very much, so I don't think I'll be cleaning for him anymore."

"Well, that's up to you," Willie supposed.

I hope you never find out what happened, Reather contemplated her dilemma.

My Mother's Black Child

After dinner, Willie went to bed early while Reather stayed up sewing. She liked to sew, because the clothes she really liked, she couldn't afford to buy, since they didn't have the money.

* * * * * *

Three months later, Reather began to feel sick a lot in the mornings. She couldn't understand why she felt tired all the time and kept vomiting. A visit to the doctor told her she was three months pregnant and the baby was due to be born in early December. Reather thanked the doctor, but inside she was very upset. *I can't be pregnant! Not now! What will I tell Willie? He knows I don't want any more children right now and this baby will probably be black too!*

Never in her deepest thoughts did Reather think that this baby was not Willie's. Then, just as she was coming out of the doctor's office, she saw Mr. H.B. He walked past her like he never saw her. Reather stopped dead in her tracks. Then she came to the realization-- *This is his baby I am carrying and why didn't I think of it before?* She knew when this baby was born Willie would know it wasn't his. *What am I going to do now?* She lamented. Deciding not to tell Willie that this was a white man's baby, she made up her mind to say the baby looked like her grandmother, Paralee. After all it could be possible.

Necholia Johnson Beck

When Willie came home that evening, Reather told him she was pregnant again but that she hadn't planned on it happening so soon.

Willie said sarcastically, "I thought you didn't want any more black kids!"

"I didn't...I mean... I don't, but it's too late now. Maybe this baby won't be real black."

"Yeah, you hope."

Reather looked at Willie disgustedly, "Oh, why don't you just shut up?"

Then Willie asked her, "How far along are you?"

"The baby is due in early December."

"Well, I just hope things will be different this time," he stated.

The next day Willie told his father and Rutha that Reather was pregnant again.

"Oh, how can she even think about having another child after the way she's done Bo?" Rutha wailed. "I just don't know about that girl!"

Shorty didn't say anything, he just looked at Willie and thought, *I hope this one won't be black for the baby's sake.*

As if to read his daddy's mind, Willie blurted out, "Maybe, she'll be a better mother this time around." Then he went outside to play with Bo, and teach him how to catch a ball. They had a good time together and Bo liked being with his daddy. Willie told Bo, "You know, little man, you are going to have a baby brother or sister soon."

Bo looked up at Willie and said, "B A B Y."

My Mother's Black Child

Willie laughed, "Yeah, Bo, B A B Y." Bo hugged his daddy and kissed him before they went inside.

Bo never did ask about his mother too much, but Rutha and Shorty knew why he didn't, so they didn't pressure him to talk about her.

* * * * * *

One week later, Dorthy stopped in to see Reather and to ask her if she was really pregnant. Dorthy had heard Reather was pregnant and was very surprised. She wanted to know for herself. They sat at the kitchen table, drinking lemonade and Dorthy asked, "Is it true, Reather? Are you pregnant again?"

"Yes, I am," Reather replied, "I'm glad and also kind of worried."

"Why?"

"Because this baby may not be Willie's."

Dorthy almost choked on her lemonade. "May not be Willie's? What do you mean?"

"I mean this baby may be white!"

"How can you have a white baby? Reather, girl, you have really lost your mind! Now to hate black so much that you have fooled yourself into thinking you are going to have a white baby?"

"No, Dorthy, I mean Mr. H.B. and I slept together one day when I cleaned his house."

"You're lying!" Dorthy accused her.

"No, I'm not. He told me I was pretty and how he wanted me and I believed him."

"I knew you were crazy, but girl! You have really done it this time," Dorthy shook her head, "How are you going to make Willie believe this baby is his if it isn't?"

"I guess I'll tell him it took color after Grandma Paralee," Reather reasoned.

"He won't believe that, Reather, and what will these white people think when they find out? Girl, you could be run out of town and they could kill your baby! Oh, my God, I hate to even think about all the things that could happen to you, Reather."

"Yeah, Dorthy, I know, but at least my baby won't be black this time."

Dorthy looked at her with disbelief, "You are too color struck, Reather, and one day you are going to pay for all of the things you've done to people, especially the way you've treated Bo."

"Ok, Dorthy, you've made your point, and I disagree, so would you please leave my house?"

"Yes, I will leave," Dorthy stated, "But you just remember what I said."

Reather cried after Dorthy left, but she really didn't care what anybody thought because she was finally going to have a light skinned baby. So what if Willie didn't like it, what could he do? Nothing and that is exactly what will happen. Nothing.

The next day Reather went over to see Bo and tried to play with her son but Bo cried

My Mother's Black Child

whenever they were alone in the room. Rutha heard him crying, and came running into the room, "What's wrong with Bo?" she asked.

"Nothing," Reather replied, "He just doesn't want to have anything to do with me."

"Bo, will you go see what Grandpa is doing?" Rutha asked.

Bo ran out of the room to find his grandpa and Rutha turned on Reather, "You have made your own child hate you by being so color struck!"

"Ok, so I won't come back to see him then. You and Mr. Shorty are teaching him against me!" Reather accused her.

"No, we are not doing that. You've done that all by yourself."

Reather left crying, and went home to tell Willie that Bo wouldn't have anything to do with her.

"No, Reather, Willie said, "You know that is not true—you treated Bo so bad when he was here until that child knows how you feel about him and you can't blame anybody but yourself."

"I know I don't like black, but Willie, I don't feel that your folks should have anything to do with that. Bo is my child and how I feel about him is none of their business," Reather continued, "Ok, I'll let them raise him and I won't go back to see him."

"You do that," Willie admonished, "And that boy will grow up hating you the rest of your life."

Necholia Johnson Beck

At that time, Reather still didn't care because her new baby would be born soon and that would show Bo and everyone else how she felt about being black.

* * * * * *

Six months passed and it was almost time for Reather's baby to be born. One day Willie came home from work very angry. He had heard from his sister Mattie, that when Reather has her baby, it was going to be white! He confronted her with that accusation and she calmly replied, "I don't know what you are talking about! This baby is ours!"

"Ok, Reather, if you are lying, I'll know if you are lying, and you had better hope the baby is black for your sake!"

"What do you mean, for my own sake?"

"I mean if this baby is a white man's, you could end up dead somewhere, not to mention what might happen to this baby. These white people here will kill you and that baby! How do you think I feel, Reather, knowing you are my wife and you have a child by a white man? I can get a divorce and leave you, but I love you and I'm going to stand by you as much as I can."

She stood quiet but her thoughts were brimming over, *I'll leave you first, and me and my baby won't need you. Then you and all of those Johnsons can go to hell for all I care.*

My Mother's Black Child

* * * * * *

On December 16, 1946, Reather gave birth to a baby girl, and Aunt Loddie, Reather's aunt delivered her. Loddie was a mid-wife in Gurdon. She told Reather, "You have a girl, and she looks white to me! What have you done?"

"This baby is white, Aunt Loddie," Reather said, "Willie isn't this baby's father. Mr. H.B. is. It happened when I used to clean house for him."

"Willie's gonna leave you for sure, now," Aunt Loddie stated.

"I don't care, Aunt Loddie, I want my baby. She's so pretty and she's light-skinned and look at her little eyes; they're blue!"

By that time, Willie had arrived home from work and wanted to see the baby.

Reather pulled the blankets back and said, "Look Willie, she is so pretty!"

Willie saw a little white baby with blue eyes and blonde fuzz for hair. He was steaming hot with anger, "Reather this baby is white! Who is this baby's father?"

"Willie, please don't ask me that," Reather pleaded.

He grabbed Reather by the hair and demanded again, "Who is this baby's father?"

"Mr. H.B. It happened one day when I used to clean house for him. I didn't mean to sleep

Necholia Johnson Beck

with him, but he forced himself on me and I couldn't stop him!"

"You're lying!" Willie shouted.

"No, Willie, please, I'm not lying."

"Yes, you are, Reather. You always wanted a light skinned baby. You even gave Bo away because he was black. I believe you wanted a white baby and I'm leaving you."

Willie left and Reather started crying. She thought, *I've got to get Willie back, but I don't know if he'll ever come back now.*

After he stormed out of the house, Willie went over to see his daddy and Rutha. He told them that Reather had the baby and it was white. Rutha and Shorty couldn't believe their ears, but they knew Willie wouldn't lie. Rutha told Willie, "I heard that his baby was Mr. H.B.'s, but I thought it was just talk. Now, I know it was true."

Shorty agreed, "She didn't want my grandbaby Bo because he was too black and now she's got a half-white baby. Well, I guess now we know how she really feels. She hates black, and I don't care if I ever see her again!"

"I know you're right, daddy," Willie said, "But I just can't leave her there all by herself. I feel like I've got to help her and that baby. The baby can't help who its' father is."

"Yeah, you're right, son, so do what you have to do. We'll stand by you."

My Mother's Black Child

Willie went into Bo's room where he was playing with his toys and sat down next to him, "Bo, mama just had a new baby today and now you have a sister."

Bo just looked up and said "B A B Y."

Willie smiled and nodded his head, "Yeah, that's right baby."

Then Bo asked, "What's baby's name?"

Willie answered, "We haven't named her yet, but I'll be back tomorrow and tell you baby's name, Ok?"

"Ok, Dad."

He left out of the room with tears in his eyes, and thought about how much he loved his son, and couldn't understand why Reather could not like him. Willie told Rutha and Shorty he was going back home to try and patch things up with Reather. Both of them just said, "Do what you feel is best."

When Willie came in the door, Reather was surprised and asked him, "Why did you come back?"

"I came back because I love you and I want to help you because you are going to need all the help you can get, now, with this baby here. What did you name her?"

"I named her after my mother Alice," Reather said.

"She sure is pretty with this little fuzz for hair," Willie replied.

Necholia Johnson Beck

They both smiled as Reather sat holding Alice.

A week later, everyone is Gurdon knew that this nigger woman, Reather Johnson, had a half-white baby and the town's pillar citizens didn't like that at all. Talk was circulating that some of them wanted her out of town and there was even a plot to kill the baby. Reather had heard the rumors about how they wanted her out of town and was afraid for her life.

One Sunday afternoon, Willie decided he would bring Bo over to see his baby sister. When they got to the house, Reather was nursing Alice. Bo ran over to where she was and said "Baby Al."

Willie laughed, "Yeah, see your little sister?"

Reather pushed Bo back and yelled at him, "No, Bo, don't touch her, you might hurt her!"

Bo just stood there and held his head down, not saying anything.

Willie intervened, "He just wanted to see her and he's not going to hurt her."

Reather looked at Bo, and then said to Willie, "I just don't want him touching her!"

Willie didn't say anything else, but thought later he would have a talk with Reather.

"I want to go home, Dad," Bo told him.

"Ok, I'll take you back." Willie was very disappointed in Reather's behavior.

My Mother's Black Child

Reather looked humiliated, but didn't say anything.

When Willie and Bo returned to Shorty and Rutha's home, Willie told Bo he would stop by tomorrow. Then he told the couple how Reather had a fit when Bo tried to touch the baby, "She acted like Bo's skin color was going to rub off on Alice."

Rutha declared, "I told you Reather hates Bo in many ways, and if I were you, I would not try to force Bo on her anymore."

Shorty on the other hand was furious over Reather's behavior, "Willie, I don't want Bo back over there any more! He's your son, but we are raising him and I'd rather he never go over there again. You can come over here and see him anytime you wish, but Bo shouldn't be around Reather until he's old enough to understand how she is."

Willie hung his head, "Daddy, I know you're right. I won't take him over there anymore."

* * * * * *

Christmas was very lonely that year without Bo home to get up early and open his Christmas presents, so Willie went over to Shorty and Rutha's to spend Christmas with Bo, his father and stepmother, his three brothers, Vernon, Jerry, Bill, his sister, Mattie and their kids. They all had a good time. Reather's name wasn't even mentioned except when Bo said, "I have a baby sister."

Necholia Johnson Beck

Mattie put her arm around Bo, "You do? That's good sweetheart."

There was an awkward silence until Jerry decided to play the harp. Then they all began to sing Christmas carols and managed to forget the sad things for a while.

Finally, the night ended with everyone going home and Willie, too, went home. Reather was in bed with Alice when he walked in. Willie was sleeping in the room that used to be Bo's. Before he went to sleep, Willie prayed, "Oh Lord, please help me. Give me strength to go on and try to make it. Take care of Bo, Lord, for I love him very much."

Two months passed and Reather decided she would go into town with Alice. Dorthy stopped by and she also decided to go with. When they got to town, Emma, Dorthy's sister, was there, so all of them went into this furniture store owned by wealthy white people to look at a bed for Alice.

Everyone stared at Reather because they knew she was the one who had a white baby. One of the clerks came over and asked Reather if she could help her.

Reather replied, "Yes, I need a baby bed."

The clerk looked at Alice while Reather was holding her and said, "Ok, we have some over here. Why don't you look around and see what you like."

By that time, Emma had noticed all these white people had huddled up and were whispering to each other. She knew they were talking about Reather. About that time, one of the other clerks

My Mother's Black Child

came over and asked Reather if she could hold her baby.

"Yes, you may," Reather said.

The clerk disappeared and Emma found her upstairs about to smother Alice with a pillow. She shouted at her, "What are you doing?"

The clerk turned to Emma, "I was going to kill her! This is a nigger baby with white blood and we don't want that kind here!"

"Give me the baby and we'll leave."

The clerk handed Alice to Emma and Emma went back to Reather, "We have to leave now," she spoke in low tones, "The clerk was trying to kill Alice and I stopped her."

Reather took Alice and ran out of the store as fast as she could.

As they were driving home, Dorthy remarked to Reather, "I told you, this would happen, but you didn't believe me and there will be a next time. What are you going to do?"

"I don't know, I guess I'll have to leave town because these people could kill both of us. What am I going to tell Willie?"

"Tell him the truth," Dorthy replied, "It's all over town, anyway. Maybe, you can go to Rockford, where Jim and Vera are."

"Yeah, that's right, Dorthy. I'll go to Rockford. Big cities aren't like that about half-white babies."

Willie was already home when Dorthy and Reather got back. They told him what happened.

Necholia Johnson Beck

"I'm not surprised. Reather, you know how these white people are and you should have known better than to take that baby around them."

"Willie, I didn't know this would happen," Reather defended herself.

"It's time for me to go," Dorthy said, "Reather, I'll see you later." And she left.

That night Willie agreed to send Reather and Alice to Rockford, Illinois, to live with Reather's brother, Jim and his wife, Vera. He would join them later.

At the same time Emma was telling her husband, Buster, about what happened to Reather earlier in town that day. There came a knock at the door. Buster looked out the window and all he could see was this white man standing there. He called out, "Who's there?"

"It's H.B.! Open this door! I want to talk to Emma."

Buster told Emma who it was and opened the door, "Come in," he said.

H.B. staggered in and declared, "Emma, I just want you and everyone else in this damn town to know that half-white baby Reather Johnson has is MINE! Anybody who don't like it can go to HELL."

Emma replied angrily, "You get out of my house and don't ever come back!"

"All right, I'll leave, but I just want you to know. I don't want no parts of Reather, but that

My Mother's Black Child

baby is MINE." H.B. left stumbling out the door and down the steps.

Buster closed the door after him, and said, "That white man has a lot of nerve to come here and say something like that."

"Well, at least he told the truth," Emma supposed. "Reather has to leave here because some of the other white people will kill her for sure, and Alice, too."

Three weeks later, Reather left on a Saturday morning, taking a train up to Rockford, Illinois. Willie was relieved that she wouldn't be in as much danger now that she was gone. As he drove away from the station, he entertained thoughts of killing Mr. H.B., *I should kill him, but no, I'd better not, that wouldn't make matters any better.* Then he thought, *Reather didn't even say good-bye to Bo, but it's probably better this way. Bo don't want to be around her anyway.* His intentions were to drive home, but he ended up at Shorty and Rutha's house.

Shorty was playing with Bo when Willie got there. Willie told Bo that mama and baby sister Alice were gone.

"Where?' Bo asked.

"On vacation," Willie answered, "They went to see your Uncle Jim and Aunt Vera in Rockford, Illinois.

"Oh, Ok, Dad," Bo replied.

Rutha asked Bo if he wanted to eat and, of course, Bo said yes, so they went off to the kitchen.

Willie and his dad talked about how they were glad Reather was gone, and then he asked Willie, "How soon are you leaving?"

Willie shrugged, "I don't know, pretty soon, I guess."

Shorty knew it wouldn't be long before Willie would be going to Rockford, too.

"What about Bo?"

"Well, I guess he can stay here with you. Reather don't want him anyway, she's got the child she always wanted."

"Ok, son," Shorty said sadly, "We will be glad to keep Bo and don't worry about him, because we'll take good care of him."

Nothing else was said about Reather. It came time for Willie to leave so he drove home. He thought about how lonesome it was there all by himself. He missed Reather, and Alice, too. He had begun to love Alice as much as he could, seeing it wasn't his child.

* * * * * *

Three months later, Willie quit his job and went to Rockford to be with Reather and Alice. They were living with Jim and Vera until Willie obtained a job at Gunite's. Gunite's was a foundry and paid good money. Willie and Reather found an apartment on Peoples Avenue, near Gunite's.

Reather began to resent Willie being around. She didn't work, so she spent everyday with Alice,

My Mother's Black Child

kept the apartment clean and made sure Willie's meals were on time. They hadn't really slept together since Willie had been in Rockford, either. That night Reather decided she would sleep with him because he had been saying she hadn't been much of a real wife lately, so they made love and a month later Reather was pregnant again. Reather didn't want anymore of Willie's babies because they would all probably be black like him! She told him she was pregnant and he was happy. Then Willie said he wanted to see Bo and that he sent Bo some money.

"Good. Go. See him then," Reather said sarcastically, "I'm not going! I don't care if I ever see that little black child again!"

Willie slapped her across the room. "Shut up!" he warned her. "Don't you ever talk about my child like that. I don't make a difference with Alice because she's half-white, so why should you talk that way about Bo? Bo is your child, too. Why can't you care about him? And now you are pregnant again! I guess if this baby is black, you'll give it away, too!"

"Yeah, I will," Reather replied.

"I'll leave you for good this time. I'm sick of you, anyway."

"Ok."

"I'll leave after this baby is born and you can do what ever you want to."

Reather didn't say anything. She was glad Willie was leaving.

A few days later Reather told her sister-in-law that she was pregnant again.

Vera asked, "Are you going to give this one away, too?"

"Oh, God! Not you, too!" Reather cried in exasperation, "I can't help how I feel about the color of my kids. I like light-skinned kids better. They are prettier."

Chapter 2

On February 12, 1948, Reather gave birth to another baby girl. She was dark, but had pretty black hair. Reather's first reaction when she first saw her new baby was: another black baby! She named her Necholia Ann Johnson.
Willie was a proud father again, passing out cigars to some of his friends. This time Reather tried really hard not to let color get in the way of caring for this baby. Bo was black and now, another black child had come along. Reather decided to call her baby girl by her middle name, Ann. Alice would play with Ann, which made Alice smile so Ann would kick her little legs. Alice didn't know the difference yet about Ann being a different color.

Willie worked five days a week at Gunite's, sometimes seven days since he needed as much overtime as he could get right now. The family had a new baby to take care of and this baby was his—this time around. He also kept in touch with Shorty and Rutha as much as possible, because he wanted Bo to know his dad hadn't forgotten about him. Deep down Willie hoped someday they could all be a family again, but that was a big HOPE.

On the weekends, when Willie didn't work, he began to drink a lot and Reather hated this. They argued all the time, which didn't stop Willie from drinking. Reather began to go out more and leave Alice and Ann with anyone who would watch them.

* * * * * *

Six months passed and Reather was going out more and more until Willie told her she needed to stay home some because it didn't look right for her to be always in the streets, leaving her kids with whoever.

"I'm not staying home all the time while you drink and act a fool!" she replied. "I need some time to myself."

"Are you sure you need time to yourself or time with someone else?" Willie baited her.

Before she had time to think about it, Reather slapped him across his face. He grabbed her arm, and threatened her, "Don't you ever do that again!"

My Mother's Black Child

"I'll put you out of here if you keep acting crazy," she countered.

"Oh, yeah? You go right ahead and I will take both those kids away from you if you push me."

"No you won't," cried Reather, "Alice isn't your child and you can have Ann. I don't care. She's too black for me, anyway!"

"Alright, now you're on your color thing again," Willie said. "Reather, you are going to regret how you feel about Bo and Ann one of these days and there won't be anything you can do."

"Who cares?" Reather laughed, "I'll give all the black kids I have AWAY if I have to and I will keep Alice, she belongs to me, not you!"

Willie retorted, "She has my last name."

"No, she doesn't," Reather coldly replied, "She don't even have a birth certificate, so you see, she doesn't have Johnson as a last name. One of these days, I will change her name when the time comes."

Willie just looked at Reather and shook his head, "You're crazy!"

The next day Reather dressed Alice up in a pretty dress, while Ann had nothing on but a T-shirt and diaper. Then she dropped the kids over to a neighbor's house and set out to see this man she had met.

Willie came home early from work. Finding Reather and the girls gone, he went next door. He told the neighbor lady he was there to get the kids and take them back home. Nine o'clock came and it was getting late, but still no Reather.

At twelve o'clock midnight, Reather came home. She knew Willie would be mad, but she didn't care, she was going to ask him to leave anyway.

Willie was asleep in the bed, but when he heard the door open, he got up. "Where have you been?" he asked.

"I've been out."

"Out where?" Willie persisted.

"With my friends," she answered him.

"You don't have any friends, except men friends you sleep around with!" he accused her.

"Ok, Willie, that is enough," Reather yelled, "You can get out! I'm sick of you anyway, so I'm asking you to pack your clothes and get out!"

At that point, Willie didn't feel like arguing further with Reather so he stated, "Ok, I'll leave in the morning."

"Take Ann with you," she called after him as he walked out of the room. "I don't want anything that belongs to you!"

"How can I take a small baby with me?" He anguished, "I don't where I'm going myself."

"If you don't take her, I'll take her to Aunt Sara to keep," Reather promised.

Willie made his mind up to leave Reather, but he didn't trust her with Ann. Reather was very mean towards Ann, and he had caught her several times beating the baby. Willie also knew that the

My Mother's Black Child

mistreatment would continue when he left. He decided to go back to Arkansas to ask his daddy and Rutha if they would take Ann until he could find a job. He would raise her himself.

The next morning, Willie packed his clothes and informed Reather that he would be back as soon as he could to get Ann. Reather agreed. He left on the morning train to Arkansas the day after. When he arrived in Gurdon, he caught a ride to Shorty and Rutha's house. Bo was outside in the yard playing and ran to meet his daddy. Willie gave him a big hug, and kiss. Then he told Bo he missed him and was home to stay. Shorty and Rutha didn't know Willie was coming home. They were surprised to see him, but understood when he explained to them what happened in Rockford with Reather. Both agreed that they would help Willie by keeping Ann, if that is what he wanted.

Willie got his old job back and started the very next day. He planned to save enough money to bring Ann home to Arkansas. His mind constantly worried about Ann because he didn't trust Reather with her. Bo was looking forward to seeing his little sister, as he would always say "See Ann! See Ann!" Over the next month, Willie kept in touch with Reather and then one day, he received a letter, stating that she had left Ann with her Aunt Sara. Sara lived in Malvern, Arkansas, which was not far from Gurdon. So, Willie decided he would go see his baby-Ann. When Willie arrived at Sara's house, she welcomed him inside, and then he saw Ann.

Her big smile told him how much he had missed her. She reached out with both arms to be picked up. Willie scooped her up and kissed her with tears in his eyes. "Sara," he stated, "I've come to get my Ann."

"I can't let you take her," Sara surprised him with her words. "Because Reather didn't tell me to let you have her."

"What do you mean, 'I can't take her'?" Willie asked. "Reather told me when we were in Rockford that she didn't want her and for me to take her with me."

"I can't do it, Willie," Sara replied, "You know how Reather can be and until I hear from her, you can't take Ann with you."

A look of sadness came over Willie. "Ok," he said finally, "I'm going to call Reather and ask her what the hell she means."

Willie concentrated on playing with Ann to ease his mind. After awhile, he left. All the way home, he contemplated his anger and how crazy Reather was.

When Willie arrived back at his dad's house, he told Shorty and Rutha that Reather had never said to Sara that he could take Ann back with him. He was going to call her right then, but before he could, Reather called Sara to tell her it was all right if Willie took Ann. Ann was just too black for Reather and she didn't want Ann. Sara wrote to Willie telling him of all that was said, so Willie made plans immediately to go and pick Ann up.

My Mother's Black Child

Willie was back at Sara's front door, all set to pick his baby up. Sara had all of Ann's clothes packed and ready. She looked at Willie, and said, "I'm sorry for not letting you take Ann before."

Willie replied, "That's Ok. Thanks for taking care of my baby.

"You know," Sara continued, "One of these days, Reather is going to regret how she's treated these children. I don't understand why she is so color struck."

Willie agreed, "I know, Miss Sara, but that is all right. Daddy and I will raise them."

Willie drove straight back to Gurdon, while Ann slept most of the way home. He marveled to see that Ann's hair had fallen out. When he last saw her, it was so pretty, black and curly. Now she hardly had any hair at all. It made him very angry. Willie couldn't decide if Reather had not taken care of Ann's hair or Miss Sarah had done something to her, but now that she was going back home with him, he knew it would grow back. He kissed her and sang to her as they drove through the night.

Ann fell asleep in the back seat and slept all the way to Gurdon. Willie had plenty of time to think while he drove and his thoughts centered on what he was going to do now that he had both of his kids with him. He knew Shorty and Rutha would help him, but he didn't want Bo or Ann think he didn't love them because of the way Reather treated them. It made him more determined to be the best father he could be. He felt it was important for his kids to know that the color of their skin didn't matter and that he would always love them no matter what. He would take care of them and raise them himself if need be. There was always Daddy and Rutha to count on for support.

Ann was beginning to wake up now and she would probably be hungry, but Willie didn't want to stop. He wanted to wait until they got home so Ann could have a good home-cooked meal. Rutha was a very good cook and he knew Ann would like that a lot. Ann had fallen back asleep so Willie decided to keep on driving. That was Ok with him because he wanted her to sleep until they got back home.

Shorty and Rutha were waiting up for him. They hugged and kissed and cried when they saw Ann. It had been such a long time. Bo heard noises and he came out to see what the commotion was. When Bo saw Ann, he kissed her and tried to hold her in his lap. Willie looked at his son, and said, "You're going to have to help Daddy and Rutha take care of your little sister.

Bo answered, "Ok, Dad. I'll help."

Rutha looked at Ann and commented, "This is such a pretty little baby. How could anyone just leave their baby and say they don't want it anymore? I will never understand Reather as long as I live."

"You're not alone," Willie responded, "I don't either."

They were all worn out and retired to bed. Willie also spent the night there with both of his

My Mother's Black Child

children. He thought about Alice and how Reather was going to raise her, but it wasn't his concern anymore. Reather was out of his life for good. Willie had his mind made up to stay and work in Gurdon so he could make a good life for his two kids. Shorty and Rutha raised Bo and Ann together.

* * * * * *

One year later, Willie got married again. This time it was to a lady named Exie Bee McCoy. They were married in Gurdon. The newlyweds stayed in Gurdon another year and then decided to move to Kansas City, Missouri. Shorty and Rutha wanted to raise Ann and Bo, so Willie agreed to let them. Willie hoped that Exie Bee would accept Bo and Ann. He hoped she would help him take care of the kids but he wouldn't force her to love them. Willie and Exie Bee would always come to Gurdon on their vacations, and between times, would send money for Bo and Ann. Shorty and Rutha never heard from Reather, she never wrote or came to see Bo and Ann. Through others, they heard Reather had married again. This time it was to a man from Chidester Arkansas, which was not very far from Gurdon. His name was Virgil Box, but people called him by his nickname, Payne. She also had another child. Rutha thought, *so Reather is supposed to be married again. Well, I hope she does better this time around.*

Necholia Johnson Beck

One day someone came to Bo and Ann's school to pay both of them a visit. Ann was in first grade and Bo was in fourth at the time. Ann was sitting at her desk and all of a sudden a lady walks into the classroom. Ann looked up and somehow, she knew this lady was her mother. The lady and her teacher, Miss Jones, hugged each other. Ann watched them, thinking, *This is my mother, I know it is!* At that moment Miss Jones said, "Ann, someone is here to see you."

Ann stood up and walked towards the lady. They went outside together. Then Bo came outside too. The lady said, "I'm your mother." She led them to a car where a little girl and a man were waiting.

"This is your little sister, Kris," Reather began. "And this is Payne Box, your stepfather."

Payne was very nice to Bo and Ann and even gave them some money. Then Reather continued, "Tell Mr. Shorty and Rutha that I'll be back tonight to see them and ask Rutha to bake some T-cakes." T-cakes were cookies that Rutha always baked and Reather loved them. Then she left. Bo and Ann went back inside to school.

When Bo and Ann got home from school that afternoon, they told Rutha and Shorty they had seen their mother at school today.

"She said she wants you to bake some T-cakes," Ann informed Rutha. "She also said she is coming back tonight."

Rutha and Shorty looked at each other and asked, "What did the lady say her name was?"

My Mother's Black Child

"Reather," Ann replied, "She said her name was Reather and that she is our mother."

Bo didn't say very much. He listened to Ann tell the story. He didn't seem too excited, but Ann, however, was very excited. She couldn't really remember her mother too much since she was very young at the time her mother left.

Shorty turned to Rutha, "I'll bet she won't come," he gruffed.

Rutha responded, "Oh, I don't know. She just might." She decided to make some T-cakes just in case. Rutha liked Reather, just didn't like the way Reather treated Bo and Ann.

Reather never did come. Shorty and Rutha waited up until ten o'clock that night, and she never showed.

"I told you she wasn't coming," Shorty commented.

"Yeah, I guess you were right," Rutha helped a sleepy Ann to bed. Bo was all ready in bed.

The next morning, Ann woke up extra early and anxiously inquired, "Did my mother come last night?"

"No, honey," Rutha soothed her, "She didn't."

Ann stood there, very disappointed, and hurt. Wistfully, she said, "Maybe they had car trouble."

"Don't worry, Ann, you will see her one day."

Ann sighed, "Ok." Then, she began to get ready for school.

Bo never did mention Reather's name. Rutha asked Bo, "How did you like seeing your mother?"

Bo's tone was very somber, "It was all right." Then he went silent. At that, Rutha could tell Bo didn't like the idea of his mother showing back up in their lives.

After the children left for school, Shorty spoke up, "I don't want Reather trying to come back to see Bo and Ann after the way she treated them."

"I know," Rutha countered, "You have a right to feel that way, but one of these days the kids are going to see their mother whether we want them to or not."

"Not if I can help it!" Shorty bellowed. "That woman ain't fit to be a mother and now she's got another child? God help her!"

Rutha didn't say anything else. That day, they got a letter from Willie. Rutha sat down and quickly composed a letter, informing Willie about Reather seeing Bo and Ann. She knew Willie would be upset, but she had to tell him.

Exie Bee wrote back to say they would be home in about two weeks and that Willie was very upset about Reather seeing Bo and Ann.

When Willie and Exie Bee arrived, Willie made it plain that in no uncertain terms Reather was not allowed in their lives until Ann and Bo were old enough to make their own minds up. It was agreed

My Mother's Black Child

amongst them that Willie was right and the subject was never mentioned again.

Willie and Exie Bee went back to Kansas City two days later. Exie Bee didn't like Ann especially. She tried, but thought Ann reminded her a great deal of Reather. Ann looked like Reather only she was darker. Bo and Exie Bee got along well. Ann always knew Exie Bee didn't like her very much, but never said anything.

* * * * * *

Later in the summer of that same year, Reather's sister, Opal, came home to Gurdon to visit her father. Ann and Bo didn't know their Aunt Opal. Opal brought Alice with her, and Alice spent the night with Ann. Ann liked her sister, but she couldn't understand why her hair was a reddish color and her eyes were green. Her braids were long and Ann thought she was a white girl. The two girls played in the hay, rode horses, and helped milk the cows. Alice enjoyed herself very much because she had never seen anything like a farm before. She lived in the city. Bo liked Alice, too, but became very quiet whenever the conversation turned to anything about his mother.

Opal returned to pick up Alice three days later, promising to see Bo and Ann the next time she was in town. Ann missed her sister after she left, but knew she would see her again someday.

Necholia Johnson Beck

The next day, Ann asked Rutha, "Why doesn't our mother want us to live with her?"

Rutha answered, "Your mother didn't want you because you and Bo were too black for her."

Ann was very surprised and hurt by this, but she now knew why she and Bo weren't living with her mother and Alice was. "Why are we black and Alice isn't?"

"Because Willie is the father of you and Bo, but he's not the father of Alice. Alice's father is someone else."

"Is he white?" Ann asked.

"Why did you ask me that?"

"Because Alice looks white and Bo and I are black."

"Well, sweetheart," Rutha chose her words carefully, "One day, you will be old enough to understand all of this, but for now, I think you are too young."

Rutha watched sadly as Ann walked away, thinking, *You don't know everything yet, but you know 'different' and how it must hurt to know your own mother doesn't want you because you are too black.*

That night, after Bo and Ann had gone to sleep, Rutha told Shorty Ann knew why Reather didn't want them.

"How does she know?" Shorty asked.

"Because I told her when she asked if Alice was white," Rutha replied.

My Mother's Black Child

"Well," Shorty answered, "They had to know someday and now is as good as any."

* * * * * *

Six months later, Shorty and Rutha decided to sell the house and land to move to Kansas City where Willie and Exie Bee lived. Rutha hated selling the place because her father had given her the place before he died, but Shorty insisted, so she did.

When they got to Kansas City, they lived with Willie and Exie Bee. Later, they would move to an apartment upstairs. Bo and Ann started school while Rutha got a job housekeeping. Shorty didn't find work. They lived there a year and a half. Ann hated her new school because it was so different than Arkansas. Bo was always coming home beat up by street gangs who didn't like him. After Shorty couldn't find work, Rutha and he decided to go back to Arkansas. Willie didn't want them to leave, but he understood that it probably was for the best.

He also hated not being able to spend time with Ann and Bo, so he promised them that he would come home as soon as possible.

That next week, Shorty, Rutha, Bo and Ann left for Arkansas. This time they decided to settle in Camden first. Rutha's sister Mona, and her husband lived there. Mona was so happy to see Rutha. She hadn't seen her in a long time. For two weeks, Mona and her husband put them up. Then, Rutha

Necholia Johnson Beck

and Shorty found a place in Gurdon, so back to Gurdon they moved. Bo and Ann started school and Shorty found a job cutting logs while Rutha did housekeeping for some white people who owned a store in Gurdon. Mrs. Doughty liked Rutha a lot and helped the family by making sure she paid Rutha a decent wage so Shorty and Rutha could afford to raise Bo and Ann the best they could. Mr. Doughty helped Shorty by giving him some part-time work around the store.

* * * * * *

Three years later, Rutha and Shorty had enough money for a down payment on another house. They were renting before and the place was getting too small. Bo and Ann could have a room of their own now. Bo was getting pretty big and he helped out around the house a lot. Ann would help Rutha with the housework.

"You're going to be a fine housekeeper and make some man a good wife," Rutha told Ann.

Ann just smiled and said, "Thanks, Aunt Boo."

Bo and Ann had started calling Rutha Aunt Boo when they were very small.

* * * * * *

One year later, Willie wrote to say that he and Exie Bee were coming home to stay. Willie

My Mother's Black Child

missed Bo and Ann so much he decided to move back home. Rutha told Ann and Bo the exciting news that their daddy was coming home to stay.

Ann was so overjoyed, she said, "I'll be glad when Dad comes home. I miss him. I wish Exie Bee was my real mother, then I could have my mama and daddy together like friends."

Rutha smiled, "Honey, your daddy loves you and Bo more than your mother could ever love you. One day, Ann, you will be able to see your mother and then you'll know for your own sake just how much love she has for you."

"Yeah, Ok, Aunt Boo."

Rutha started to cook supper and nothing else was said about Reather.

Bo would never talk about his mother to anyone. It was almost as if she was dead as far as he was concerned. Ann would daydream about her mother and wondered if she would ever see her. She could not understand how their own mother could just give them up because they were too black for her. Ann thought, *A mother is suppose to love her children no matter what color they are.* It would hurt her a lot to think about this and sometimes, she would even cry about it when no one else was around to see her weep.

The next week Willie and Exie Bee came home. Ann was so glad to see her father that she hugged and kissed him til he hugged and kissed her back. She was very different acting around Exie Bee since she knew Exie Bee didn't like her too much. It was that Exie Bee thought Ann reminded her of Reather a lot except that Reather was lighter skinned. So she just said, "Hi," and that was all. Bo was glad to see Willie and Exie Bee, too. Bo and Exie Bee got along fine. His stepmother would always talk to Bo and give him money.

Ann asked, "Where are you and Exie Bee going to stay?"

"Well, baby," her father replied, "We're going to stay with daddy and Rutha for now until we can find a place and move into it."

Ann brightened at that, "All right," she enthusiastically beamed, "That sounds good to me."

Willie and Exie Bee stayed for two weeks and then they found a place. They decided to move into Exie Bee's fathers' house since he had died some years ago and the house was empty. It needed a lot of work. Willie was going to fix the place up in his spare time. Ann asked Exie Bee if it would be all right if she spent some nights over and Exie Bee knew she couldn't refuse her because Willie would get upset so she said, "Yes, Ann, you are more than welcome to stay over any time you want and that goes for you, too, Bo."

Bo looked at her, "I'll think about it."

On weekends Ann would stay with Willie and Exie Bee. Ann liked staying with her daddy because she knew how much he loved her. Exie Bee pretended to get along with Ann as well as she could because to do differently would make Willie angry.

My Mother's Black Child

* * * * * *

Two years later, Reather started harassing Willie, by making threats about getting custody of Ann. Willie told her, "That last time you called you gave Bo and Ann away because you said you didn't want them because they were too black for you! Now you have the nerve to call and tell me you want her back?"

"Willie," Reather pleaded, "I'm sorry. I was wrong but I want to see Ann."

"What about Bo?" Willie asked her, "You haven't mentioned him, don't you want to see him, too?"

"No, I just want to see Ann. Bo is older, now and he's probably made his mind up that he don't want to see me."

"Reather," Willie sighed, "I can't let you see Ann. She is living with Daddy and Rutha. They love both of the kids, unlike you."

"Ok, Willie, Reather promised, "But one day I will get my chance."

Willie slammed the phone down and was extremely angry.

The next evening Willie went to tell Shorty and Rutha what Reather had said. They both agreed with his decision and could not understand how Reather could have the nerve to want to see Ann, but not Bo. Ann overheard all that was said and she thought, *do I really want to see my mother?* She thought about it hard all night long. Bo never said a word while they were talking about Reather. He never showed any feelings one way or the other.

The next day Ann went to school as usual; but all of her thoughts were on the fact her mother wanted to see her after all these years. She still couldn't make up her mind. She also couldn't ask Bo what he thought because he acted as if he hated her. So she tried to put it out of her head the rest of the day. When Ann came home from school, Rutha told her she wanted to talk to her about her mother.

"Ann," she started, "We all want you to know that we are not trying to stop you from seeing your mother, we just feel that when you are old enough to understand and make your own mind up, then we'll let you see your mother. For now, you are too young. Maybe later."

Ann looked at Rutha and slowly chose her words, "Ok, I know and I understand why all of you feel that way. I don't think you are wrong. I think you are right. It has to be my decision, but I can't make my mind up yet. Thanks. I needed to know that."

Rutha gave Ann a big hug, "We love you and we want you to be happy."

Ann smiled back and proceeded to help get supper ready.

Later that evening, Bo told Shorty and Rutha he wanted to quit school and start work.

My Mother's Black Child

"You are only seventeen!" Shorty yelled at him. "You should try and finish school first before working a job."

Bo was very serious and argued the point until finally, Shorty told him, "You'll have to talk to Willie about this, and if he says it is Ok, then, when school is out, you can quit and start work."

Bo agreed to do that, "OK, I'll talk to Dad."

Nothing else was said after that. Bo knew Willie would probably let him quit school if he really wanted to work.

That weekend, Willie came over and Bo asked him if he could quit school and go to work. Willie was upset, but Bo sounded so convincing until Willie gave in and threw up his hands, saying, "Ok, but I hope you know what you are doing."

"Dad," Bo told him, "I know what I'm doing and I really think this will be best for me."

"What about not being able to get a better paying job later?" Willie questioned.

"I feel I can do this and make it without a high school diploma," Bo said adamantly.

"Yeah, you can. Although, son, nowadays, a person needs to finish school in order to get a decent paying job. I know I said yes and good luck, son." Willie knew Bo had already made up his mind and there was no going back on his word.

* * * * * *

Necholia Johnson Beck

When summer came, Bo quit school and started driving a tractor for Sam Stephen, one of the neighbors. They worked in the woods cutting trees down for logs. Bo got to be good friends with Sam's sons, Johnny and J.N. On weekends, Bo would go out with Johnny to a place called Marine's. Marine's served drinks, food and gambling on the side. Bo liked that, and Marine liked having Bo there. She had known Bo since he was just a baby and told Shorty that she would watch over him and make sure he wouldn't get into any trouble. Marine's sold beer, wine and whiskey illegally since Gurdon was a dry county. The police made frequent visits to see what was going on and to make their presence known.

Payne Box also came back to visit his hometown that summer. He stopped by to see Ann and Bo. The kids liked him and he, in turn, liked them. Reather didn't accompany Payne on this trip. Ann always wondered why her mother would never come to see them, but she didn't dare ask.

Willie Jean, Ann's first cousin, also stopped in from Milwaukee that summer with her mother, Elga. Jean was Jerry's daughter. Willie's brother, Jerry and Elga were divorced years ago and they had one child together. Ann and Elga got along good together so Ann went back with them to spend the rest of the summer in Milwaukee.

Shorty and Rutha told Elga to make sure she took good care of Ann and for her to write. After Ann had been in Milwaukee a week, the phone rang

My Mother's Black Child

one night. Elga told Ann the phone was for her and that Reather wanted to speak with her. Ann was very surprised and really didn't know what to say to her mother. Reather told Ann she was coming over the next day to see her. All Ann could do was mumble "Ok," and hang up.

Elga told Ann not to worry because she wouldn't let Reather take her away. That night all Ann could think about was her mother. *What will she look like? Will she be pretty? Will she like me? Maybe she won't come...* the thoughts were racing through her mind.

The next morning, however, there came a knock at the downstairs door. This tall, light skinned, pretty lady came up the stairs. She was wearing a black suit and Ann thought, *there she is, this has got to be my mother!*

Elga hugged Reather and introduced her to Ann. "Ann, this is your mother."

Ann just stood there, scared, cold chills running up and down her body. Finally, she stammered, "Hi."

Reather walked over and hugged Ann. With tears in her eyes, she said, "Hello, baby."

They walked into the kitchen and sat down. Reather asked Ann to go back to Rockford with her for the weekend. Ann shook her head and said, "No, I can't."

Reather cried, "Mr. Shorty and Rutha and Willie have taught you against me!"

Necholia Johnson Beck

"No," Ann explained, "I can't go with you because I don't really know you. I know you're my mother but I can't go back to Rockford with you."

Elga also spoke up, "I wouldn't let Ann go even if she wanted to."

Reather was indignant. "Why not?"

"Because Mr. Shorty and Rutha wouldn't want me to and Willie certainly doesn't want Ann with you and I think you know why!"

Angrily, Reather huffed, "Ann is my child, too, and I have a right to see her."

"Reather," Elga stated, "You gave Bo and Ann away years ago because they were too black for you. Now, here you are, trying to come back into their lives, and not once have you asked about Bo!"

"Well, Bo's older now and he probably really hates me by now, anyway."

"You couldn't blame him if he did," Elga declared.

"No," countered Reather, "But one day, Ann will want to visit me and when that day comes, I'll see what all of you say then!"

"Reather, that's enough. I've heard all I care to hear from you and now, it's time you left my house."

"Ok, Elga, but you just remember what I've said! Good-bye!" With that Reather stomped out the door and down the stairs.

Ann was outside when Reather stormed by, "I hope one day you'll change your mind to come

My Mother's Black Child

and visit me. You have three other sisters besides Alice. Their names are Patricia, who is nine years old, Phyllis, who is five, and Roberta, the baby, who is four years old. So, please Ann, remember, you are always welcome to come anytime you want."

Ann just stood there looking sad, and softly said, "Ok, I'll remember."

All day long, Ann thought about what Reather had said, but still couldn't understand why Reather had come back into her life after so many years.

The next day, Ann wrote home to Rutha and Shorty. She informed them that Reather had come to see her. She also wrote that she was more confused than ever, and didn't quite understand all of it.

Three days later, Rutha got her letter. She read it aloud to Shorty and Willie. They both got furious. Shorty couldn't understand how Reather could do such a thing and Willie agreed.

"Why don't you let us adopt Ann and Bo so this woman of a mother can't try anything else?" Shorty asked Willie.

"Daddy, I can't do that legally, but I will find out what I can do."

"What do you mean you can't do that legally?"

"Reather is still their legal mother since she hasn't signed any papers giving me total custody of Bo and Ann, so I'll have to talk to my lawyer, Dick Jackson about it."

Necholia Johnson Beck

"Ok, son," Shorty replied, "You know best."

The next day Willie went to talk to Dick Jackson about letting Rutha and Shorty adopt Bo and Ann. Mr. Jackson informed Willie, that he couldn't do anything without Reather's consent and advised him not to do anything unless Reather made waves. Willie felt helpless but thanked Dick for his time and left.

He stopped by Shorty and Rutha's on his way home, and repeated what his lawyer had said. They decided to wait and see what, if anything, was going to happen next.

* * * * * *

The summer that year seemed so short. Ann came home from Milwaukee, and Bo continued to work. School started in September, and all seemed to be going well until late February, when Reather called. She stated she was sick and wanted to see Ann. Ann told Willie, Shorty and Rutha that she wanted to go. Reluctantly, they said Ok.

Ann left that Saturday morning to go to Rockford. When she arrived she found Reather had lied. She was not sick but had just wanted to see her. Reather also told Ann she couldn't go back to Gurdon. Ann was as surprised as much as she was hurt and scared, she didn't know what to do. She cried and cried, finally writing home to say she would be staying in Rockford to finish school there the rest of the year. This was a big mistake, Ann

My Mother's Black Child

knew, but she thought she'd give it a try for a while anyway.

Chapter 3

Ann started junior high at Lincoln Park Middle school, in the fall. She was in eighth grade now and school in Rockford was very different. She had all white teachers and most of her classmates were white, too. There were Negro kids, but not very many and not at all like school in Gurdon. Ann liked school at Lincoln Park and she especially liked the idea of the teacher giving her a new first name. Ann's gym teacher decided to call her Nicki. She thought Necholia was too hard to pronounce, so she decided to call Ann, Nicki for short. The other kids started to call her Nicki, too.

My Mother's Black Child

Ann went home and told Reather her new name was Nicki.

Reather said, "Ok, but I'm still calling you Ann." She didn't like anything that Ann liked because she wanted Ann to feel stupid, and helpless.

Ann had one friend at school and this girl lived close-by. Her name was Patricia Brown. Ann and Pat would spend a lot of time together She called Ann, Nicki, because she liked that name better. At least Reather finally let her be friends with someone.

Payne Box, Reather's husband, liked the name Nicki, too. He told Reather he liked the name and Reather got mad at him.

"Shut up!" she hissed at him.

He just laughed at her.

Her sister, Kris, whose real name was Patricia called her Nicki. So did everyone else for that matter, everyone, except Reather. But Ann didn't care if Reather didn't like her new name because she liked it and that was all that mattered.

Getting used to having little sisters was also new to Ann, because she had never had that before. It was just Bo and her back home. Alice and Ann got along well and Ann really liked her but one day Alice and Reather got into a big argument over Alice staying out too late. Reather told Alice she was going to lock her out if she wasn't home by 10 o'clock that evening.

Alice yelled, "I'm going to move out!"

"Get out then!" Reather screamed back.

Alice went into her bedroom and started packing her clothes. She declared to Ann, "You are going to hate the day you ever came here! Mama isn't like what you've probably dreamed about."

Ann just stood in the doorway and began to realize Alice was most likely right. *What was she going to do now?* She thought to herself. *Here Alice was only fifteen years old and her mother had told her to get out. What kind of a mother would tell her fifteen year old to get out?*

Alice left and Ann decided that she was going back to Arkansas as soon as school was out. She wrote Rutha and Shorty the next day to send her fare when school was over. Ann didn't quite know how she was going to break the news to Reather that she was going back to Arkansas. Reather would be furious, but she couldn't stay with her any longer.

* * * * * *

Two months passed, and Ann was really homesick now, eager to get home to Arkansas. One Sunday evening about three days before school let out, she overheard Reather and Payne say that Elbert Simms, Reather's cousin, was going to Arkansas that very weekend. Ann formed a plan to ask Elbert if she could ride with him to Arkansas. She waited until the next day while Reather was at work and called Mr. Simms.

My Mother's Black Child

"I'm Reather's daughter," Ann began, "I heard you are going to Arkansas. Can I ride along with you?"

"Why, of course, you can!" Elbert replied. "I'm leaving Friday evening and I'll pick you up then."

As Ann hung up the phone, she felt both relieved and anxious. *I'm so glad, but how am I going to tell Mama? I know, I'll tell her the day before I leave.*

School was out the next day, and Ann had passed to ninth grade. She would be in Junior High school. Ann wrote Rutha, that she would be home on Saturday and she would be riding with mama's cousin, Elbert Simms.

Thursday evening, Ann told Reather of her plans to go back to Arkansas. Reather got very angry, and declared, "I'm sorry, but I'm not paying for you to go back down to Arkansas!"

"You don't have to pay for me to go back because I'm riding with Elbert."

"With Elbert?" Reather was flabbergasted.

"Yes, with Elbert," Ann replied defiantly, "I heard you and Payne talking about it so I called him and asked him if I could ride down there with him and he said yes!"

"Well," Reather ranted, "I just want you to know if you leave, don't come back! You can stay in Arkansas if you want to, in all that heat and keep getting blacker! I would never stay down there again. I finally got your skin looking much lighter now and you want to go back. Go ahead, I don't care!"

Ann was so hurt, she started to cry. "Well," she sobbed, "I guess I'll start packing."

When Ann had left the room, Payne chided Reather, "You shouldn't have said those things to Ann."

"I don't care," Reather retorted, "I really don't want her back if she leaves!"

She finished packing her suitcase, and hoped the next day would come quickly.

Friday morning Ann got up early and got ready for Elbert. She waited all day long, but Elbert never arrived, so she decided to call him to see if he had left yet. There was no answer at his house and Ann figured out that he had left without coming to pick her up, but she didn't know why.

Reather came home from work that evening and Ann told her that Elbert didn't come.

"I know," Reather coldly replied, "I told him not to!"

But why?"

"Because you don't need to go back to Arkansas to get blacker and blacker!"

"Mama, that was very wrong of you to do something like that! I'm going with or without your help."

Reather ignored Ann's comments except to ask, "Did you use your cream today?"

"Yes, I did."

My Mother's Black Child

"Well, you need to start using it on your arms more, because, your face and neck is lighter than your arms."

Ann shook her head. *That is all she cares about. If I'm light enough for her! I'm going to write home and tell Aunt Boo and Grandpa to send my fare and I'll go home on the bus!*

The next day Ann mailed a letter to Rutha and Shorty, explaining what Reather had done. She asked for bus fare home.

Rutha received Ann's letter, three days later. She informed Shorty and Willie what Ann had been through, and they sent the money off the same day. Willie was furious.

Shorty just stated, "Now she knows how Reather really is."

"Yeah, Ann thought she knew Reather, but she found out she didn't know Reather at all."

Reather was at work when the mail came. Ann opened Rutha's letter and there was the bus fare home.

That Friday, Ann told Reather that she was going back to Arkansas and had her bus fare.

Reather angrily stated, "You don't have to go back. You should stay. Mr. Shorty and Rutha have taught you against me!"

"No Mama," Ann insisted, "That's not true. Dad nor Grandpa, nor Aunt Boo ever taught Bo or me against you. They only told the truth."

"And what was that?" Reather haughtily demanded.

"That we, Bo and I, were too black for you! That's why you gave us away!"

Shocked that her own daughter would say such a thing, Reather was indignant, "That's a lie! I didn't give you and Bo away because you were too black! Your daddy and Mr. Shorty took you away from me and told me not to try to see either one of you, so I did just that until I couldn't stand it any longer!"

Ann looked at her with disgust, "I don't believe you," she said. "Since the very first day I came here, all you've talked about is how black my skin is and made me use bleaching cream so I could be light like you want me to be!"

Reather was totally speechless. She stood there while Ann left the room crying. For the next two days, Reather and Ann didn't talk to each other at all. Saturday came and Ann packed her clothes again in order to leave the next day. *Finally, I'm going home, this time. It's not a trick, like before. I'm really going home at last.*

On Sunday afternoon, Ann left. Payne and Reather took Ann to the bus station. Reather told Ann that she never wanted her to come back and she could stay in Arkansas for the rest of her life if she wanted to!

Ann simply said, "Ok, I will stay and I won't come back!"

At that point Reather had lost all hold on her child, and she knew it. She cried while Ann boarded the bus bound for Gurdon, Arkansas.

My Mother's Black Child

Sitting on the bus, Ann had time to ponder, *I sure am glad I left there, but I hope Reather will someday learn to accept me for what and who I am, that is, black and proud of it.*

When she arrived in Gurdon late on Monday night Shorty and Rutha met her at the bus station.

Shorty was the first to greet her, "Baby, I'm so glad you're back," he said, tears welling up in his eyes.

Rutha hugged Ann, "Welcome, back," she said as her eyes started to fill up, too.

Ann smiled and expressed deep gratitude for being back with her family, "It's nice to be back home." Then, she noticed Willie was not there, and asked, "Where is Dad?"

Rutha answered, "Oh, he had to work late and said to tell you he would see you tomorrow."

Ann looked disappointed, and said, "Ok."

The next day, Willie went to see Ann. He hugged her and bawled, "Baby, I'm so glad to have you back safe and everything."

"Dad, I missed you so much and I love you."

Willie felt such strong emotion as he wept tears of joy, "Yes, Baby, and I love you, too."

Chapter 4

It was five years later, and Ann was now a senior in High School. In early May of that year, Ann was chosen one of many contestants in a Beauty Contest at her High School. She won that contest and was crowned Miss Bronze Clark County. Never in her wildest dreams did Ann ever think this would happen to her, but it did and she cried, thinking this was the happiest she had been in her life.

Three weeks later, on May 26, 1966, Ann graduated from High School. Reather came home that one time to see Ann graduate. A lot of things had changed between Ann and Reather. It was the past after all, and Ann decided she would go back

My Mother's Black Child

with her to Rockford, maybe to find a job and get her own apartment.

Well, Ann did find a job. She was an elevator operator in a large department store in downtown Rockford. But some things never change. Ann and Reather still had trouble getting along because Reather insisted that Ann bleach her skin. So to try and please her, Ann used the bleaching cream. Reather would make Ann pay rent and give her three younger sisters an allowance.

When Ann turned nineteen, she moved out of her mother's house, and in with Alice. Ann had her own furniture, and her own phone. Little did she know that Alice would end up using her, too. For about six months, Ann lived with Alice. By this time, Alice had two small children, Lisa and Angela. Lisa's father lived in California. Angela's father lived with them.

The day before Ann moved out, Reather paid a visit to Alice.

"Why didn't you tell me who my father was and that he was white?" Alice demanded.

Reather looked shocked, "I did tell you, Alice. Your father is Booker Washington. I don't know where you got the idea that your father is white."

"I just wanted to know who he is!"

"I told you Alice, Booker is your father," Reather insisted.

Ann stood, listening to all that was said, without saying a word.

Necholia Johnson Beck

Then Reather looked at Ann. "Ann, why did you tell Alice that?"

"I didn't tell Alice anything Alice didn't already know and what do you want, anyway?"

Changing the subject, Reather said, "Birdie said you hit her yesterday before you moved over here and wouldn't let her use the phone."

"I didn't do anything to Birdie. She's lying!" accused Ann.

Birdie interrupted, "Yes, you did, too."

"Well," Reather sneered, "I just want to let you know that you better leave my baby alone!"

Alice and Ann gave each other a surprised look, but neither said anything.

Ann didn't see Reather anymore for a long time after that. She would never call or visit her. There were a lot of things Ann remembered about Reather, like how she used to accuse her of stealing money out of her purse, which Ann didn't do. Reather also used to say that when her and the three kids lived there, this or that never happened. Those words really hurt Ann and made her feel like she wasn't Reather's child. Ann never found out who it was that stole the money, but she knew it wasn't her.

* * * * * *

Ann decided to moved into her own apartment when Alice ran her phone bill up to two hundred dollars and wouldn't pay any money on the

My Mother's Black Child

bill. There was a nice apartment for rent near downtown where she worked and it was there she met her first true love. Ann also started introducing herself to people by the name her Lincoln Middle School gym teacher had given her, Nicki.

The apartment that Ann lived in also had a laundromat on one side. One day, Ann was going to wash clothes and there stood this tall dark, bald-headed man next to a black Volkswagen. She was in a hurry because the machine her clothes were in was done by now and she wanted to put them in the dryer before all the dryers were taken. Ann bumped into this man and he looked up.

"Oh, I'm sorry," she gushed, "I didn't mean to bump into you like that."

Instead of getting angry, the man smiled, "That's Ok. You look like you are in a rush."

"Yes, I am," Ann said, "I mean I was in a rush to get my clothes out of the washer and into the dryer before they are all taken."

Then the man asked, "What's your name?"

"It's Nicki, Nicki Johnson. What's yours?"

"RC Pettigrew," he replied. "Well, Nicki, do you live around here?"

"Yes, Ann said, "I do. I live on one side of the laundromat in this building."

"I have a friend who lives here, too. She lives upstairs. Her name is Rose Jenkins, do you know her?"

Ann said, "Yes, I know her," and started walking away, thinking it was about time she found a dryer for her clothes.

About that time, Rose walked up and said, "Well, hello, RC Pettigrew, what are you doing over here?"

"I just met a friend of yours, Rose. Her name is Nicki."

"Oh really?" Rose gave a sly smile.

"Yes, she's a very cute dark girl. I'd like to get to know her better. Why don't you talk to her for me? I'll make it worth your while if you would do that for me," RC promised.

"Ok," Rose said, "I'll talk to Nicki and see what she says, then I'll let you know."

RC nodded his head, "Ok." And he left.

Later that evening, Rose went downstairs to talk to Nicki. Rose knocked on the door, "Nicki, are you in there?"

"Yes, Rose, I'm putting clothes away."

"Girl, I saw RC today and he wants to know when he can come and see you."

Nicki looked surprised, "RC, who?"

"You know, bald headed RC Pettigrew."

"Oh, him. I forgot. Yes, I met him today outside standing by his cute little car. He's kinda nice looking but I don't know anything about him. Is he married?"

"No," Rose said, "I think he used to go with this other girl but they broke up."

"Where does he work?" Nicki asked

My Mother's Black Child

"RC works in Belvidere at a foundry," Rose answered.

Nicki thought about it for a minute, "Ok, Tell him, yes, he can come and see me sometime."

"All right, I'll tell him." Then Rose left.

For the next few hours, Nicki could think of nothing but this man, RC Pettigrew. *What's he really like? Would he like her?* She couldn't stop wondering the answers to these questions.

All of a sudden there was a knock on the door. Nicki wasn't expecting company, so it took her by surprise. She went to the door and there stood RC. Shyly, she smiled and said, "Come in."

RC walked in and said, "Rose told me that it was Ok if I stopped by to see you." He grinned.

"Yes, I did tell her that after she said you wanted to see me again."

"You have a nice place here," RC stated, looking around. "Do you live here alone?"

"Yes, I certainly do. I work downtown at Carson, Pirie Scott and Company."

"What do you do there?"

"I'm a sales clerk."

"What department do you work in?"

"I'm in jewelry," Nicki said, then she turned the tables on him, "Now, where do you work?"

"I work in a foundry in Belvidere. It's called National Grey Iron. Tell me, Nicki, what's a nice looking girl like you doing here all alone? Where is your man?"

"I don't have a man," Nicki stated flatly.

They both just looked at each other and smiled.

RC asked, "Do you like to eat fish?"

"Yes, I do," came the reply.

"Do you mind cooking fish if I buy it?"

"No."

"Then let's go buy fish. What kinds do you like?"

"Well, I don't like catfish."

"That's Ok, we can get another kind."

So Nicki and RC left in his car. As they were driving along, Nicki thought this was the perfect guy for her! He seemed so witty and intelligent. That was not something she had found in other guys. They picked out their choices and came back to Nicki's apartment to cook. She got started in the kitchen and RC watched. Later, they sat on the couch, listening to music, and drinking wine. RC even helped Nicki wash dishes and when before he left, he asked if he could see her again. Nicki had no hesitation about saying, "Yes."

The courtship between RC and Nicki blossomed as the months passed. RC would take her out to the best places and they went to Chicago a lot. One Saturday, however, Nicki went out to buy a carton of milk and just as she got closer to the store, she saw a black Volkswagen that looked similar to RC's. Nicki waited for a few seconds, then she walked over to the car. There sat RC. Nicki was surprised and really didn't know what was going on.

My Mother's Black Child

RC looked up and saw Nicki standing there, "Hi, Nicki." He didn't seemed upset or anything.

"Hi, RC," Nicki said, "What are you doing here?"

"I just brought a lady friend to the store," He replied nonchalantly.

"Really?" She began to feel flush.

"I'll come by later and talk to you."

"That will be fine," Nicki replied, and turned to walk inside the store to get the milk. She bumped into the lady friend of RC's. Neither said anything, but awkwardly smiled at each other. Then the lady got back into the car and RC drove away.

He came by later that night and tried to explain to Nicki that he was married and the woman she saw was indeed his wife. Nicki sat there and couldn't believe her ears. Tears rolled down her cheeks. "Why didn't you tell me a long time ago that you were married?" she sobbed.

"Nicki, I just couldn't tell you I was married because you never would have agreed to see me."

"How long have you been married?" Nicki angrily asked.

"I've been married five years, but I am not in love anymore. We have two kids together, a girl and a boy."

Nicki was almost hysterical, screaming and crying at the same time. "Why? Why? Why me?"

"I don't know!"

"Why couldn't you have left me alone?"

"Nicki," RC's voice was pleading now.

Necholia Johnson Beck

"GET OUT! RC, just get the hell out of here!" Nicki shouted at him.

There wasn't anything RC could say that would make Nicki understand. So RC left and Nicki felt like her whole world had ended. She loved RC more than anyone else she had ever known. *Here was a man that not only was he handsome, but also smart, witty, and very intelligent. He knew something about anything a person wanted to know and I find out he is married. Now, I don't know what I'm going to do. I love him so much and he's the only person that made me feel good about myself.*

The phone rang almost all night and Nicki wouldn't answer it because she knew it was RC and she didn't want to talk to him. The next few days were hard ones for Nicki. She couldn't keep her mind on too much of anything besides RC.

One day, Nicki went to work and the phone rang in her department. She answered it, and a voice said, "Hi Nicki, this is RC."

Irritated, Nicki snapped, "What do you want?"

"I'd like to come by and talk to you, if that is Ok. There is a lot I need to tell you." RC begged her.

Nicki paused, and then she said, "Ok, there's a lot I also need to say but I work tonight until nine o'clock. If that is fine, I'll see you then."

"I'll pick you up tonight," RC promised.

RC was true to his word and picked Nicki up from work that night.

My Mother's Black Child

Nicki got into the car and cautiously said, "Hi."

RC responded, "Hi, Nicki."

They went back to Nicki's apartment. Once inside, Nicki turned to him and demanded, "Ok, RC, what's up?"

RC looked into her eyes, and said, "Nicki, I care a lot about you. I think you are cute, and very intelligent. I don't want to end this relationship on a note like this. I would like to continue seeing you and I plan on getting a divorce. I don't know when because of my kids and I own some property. I don't want to lose everything. I will take care of you financially and I'll spend as much time with you as I have been, but I'm still married."

Nicki was taken back and didn't know what to say or do. At this point she knew she still loved RC and wanted to be with him. He walked over to her and kissed her. Nicki put her arms around his neck and they kissed each other again passionately. "Yes," she said, "But I don't like doing this because it is wrong. I do still love you, so let's see where this will go." Nicki had given in.

RC spent the night and they made love like never before. She could feel just how much RC had missed her and was very happy to be in his arms again. The next morning, Nicki cooked breakfast and they ate in bed. RC left early and Nicki went to work.

* * * * * *

Months passed as Nicki and RC got closer than ever. One weekend, RC told Nicki he was going to Indiana to see his parents and asked her if she would like to go with him.

"I can't go," Nicki said.

"Why?" RC asked her.

"Your parents will know I'm not your wife and what will they think?"

"There is nothing for them to think. You'll be with me and they will accept that and welcome you." RC was adamant.

Nicki thought more about going to Indiana with RC, but decided against it. "It isn't the right thing to do," she stated firmly, "No, I can't go, not while you are still married."

RC shrugged and said, "Ok, I'll see you when I get back." Then he left.

She would miss him, but she thought, *it'll only be for a few days and I'll be Ok.*

While RC was gone, Nicki also thought about trying to get a job with the airlines as a stewardess. She wanted to fly and lately that was all she thought about. There was also the color of her skin to consider, which meant she might not get accepted. Nicki thought she was too dark to get a job like that. She also hadn't heard from Reather in quite a while, and that was fine with her since all she ever talked about was how she didn't like dark-skinned people. At that point, Nicki made up her mind to talk to RC about trying to get a job with the

My Mother's Black Child

airlines, to see what he thought of the idea. RC was a medium brown skinned black man. He has never acted in any way that made her think skin color was an issue. She admired him for that quality. RC will tell me the truth about how this world will treat me as a dark skinned person.

RC came back three days later and called Nicki. He told her he would see her shortly. She couldn't wait to tell him about her new job plans. She hoped he would be happy for her, because if she did get a job with the airlines, it meant she would have to leave him, but he could come to visit her wherever she would be living.

When RC arrived at Nicki's, she kissed him. He said, "I missed you terribly. I wish you would have went with me."

"RC," Nicki said slowly, "I've got something to talk to you about and I need your honest opinion."

"I want to be an airlines stewardess, but I don't think I can get accepted because I may be too dark skinned and the airlines may not hire me. I need to know from someone else what my chances are of being hired therefore, I'm asking your opinion. What do you think?" Nicki was all out of breath from talking.

RC looked at Nicki like she was crazy, "Why don't you think they will hire you because of your skin color?" he asked.

"Well, because my mother always thought I was too black for her so I thought the airlines may feel the same way. My mother used to make me bleach my skin with bleaching cream from the first time I lived with her. You see, my mother didn't raise my brother or me. She gave us away to my Dad and grandparents at two years old because we were too black for her."

RC looked astonished, "Your mother is crazy as hell, and I don't think you are too dark. You shouldn't feel that way either. You are a very pretty young lady and I think you should go for it. Sit down and write letters to the airlines. Tell them what you have to offer and I'm sure you will get the job if you try hard enough."

Nicki was grateful that RC supported her decision. "Thanks so much for believing in me," she said.

The next day Nicki was on her lunch hour at work and was reading the paper. In one section there was this huge ad for airlines stewardesses with American Airlines at the Faust Hotel the next night at 7:00pm. Nicki showed the ad to another girl at work. The next night Rita and Nicki went to the hotel and filled out applications. They were told that if they were accepted, they would get a letter within ten days.

Ten days passed. Neither Nicki nor Rita received a letter. Nicki decided to write to some other airlines. She wrote one to American again hoping this time she would hear something. RC encouraged her and told her not to give up hope.

My Mother's Black Child

She never gave up and just knew it would happen one day.

* * * * * *

Three months later, Nicki received a letter from American Airlines for an interview in Chicago, Illinois, on October 19, 1969 at ten o'clock that morning. Nicki was so excited about her interview until she thought she would burst. RC was equally excited for her. She went out and bought a new outfit, purse and shoes to match, and she read about the do's and don't for a successful interview.

On October 19th, Nicki went to Chicago on the bus for her interview. The strangest thing happened because the same man who interviewed her in Rockford, was there to interview her again in Chicago. His name was Mr. Bauer and he asked if she'd ever applied with American before. Nicki said, yes it was in Rockford, about a year ago.

After the interview, Mr. Bauer told Nicki not to cut her hair anymore and to send in a copy of her birth certificate. It all had to be back to him by the following Wednesday. When Nicki left, she was floating on air. She felt she was finally accepted this time because he didn't say anything like that before. Nicki couldn't wait to tell RC and some of her friends.

When she returned from Chicago, RC was met her at the bus station. She told him the thrilling news and he said, "You finally did it! I told you that you could do it!" Then he kissed her.

The next few days were a blur to Nicki. She sent the copy of her birth certificate like Mr. Bauer had told her to.

Nicki called Reather and told her she had used her address for mailing purposes and that American Airlines may be sending her some mail to that address. If that happened, could she let her know? Reather said she would let her know. She also said she was happy for Nicki, but Nicki knew Reather's tone indicated she was jealous. Reather always liked the idea of Nicki being down and never being able to accomplish anything good in life.

On Wednesday, Reather called and informed Nicki she had a letter from American Airlines. When she got there, Reather gave her the letter and Nicki opened it right there.

It read: Welcome to American Airlines.

She told Reather what was in the letter, and Reather responded, "I'm happy for you."

"Thank you," Nicki replied and then she left.

RC came over that night and Nicki showed him the letter. On April 11, 1969, Nicki had to be at American Airlines, Dallas-Fort Worth Stewardess College in Texas. That left only six months before Nicki was to leave.

* * * * * *

My Mother's Black Child

During that six-month period, RC made sure he wined and dined Nicki a lot. He took her to all the best places and they made a lot of love. Making love with RC was better than ever now, maybe because Nicki knew she was leaving and felt as though she had to make up for the all the time they were going to lose.

She gave up her apartment and moved in with Alice for a while. And she gave her furniture to RC, with the stipulation that if she ever needed furniture again, he would buy it for her.

After some time, Nicki decided to move from Alice's place to live with her friend, Doris. They had met while Nicki worked at Rockford Dry Goods. The apartment Doris had was also closer to work and that was better. Nicki and Doris had a lot in common and they like each other's company. They would stay up late and talk. It was fun. Besides, RC liked Doris, too. He would spend the night occasionally and that was Ok with Doris.

* * * * * *

It was late March now, and Nicki hadn't started her period for this month, yet. She hoped she wasn't pregnant, but she was beginning to get worried. *That's all I need now, to get the job I've always wanted, and then have something like this happen to me. I've got to tell RC just in case I am pregnant and see what we can do,* she thought.

The next afternoon, Nicki told RC what she felt.

"If you are pregnant, you can have the baby or get an abortion," He told her.

Nicki thought about what he had said. Then she dismissed her fear as nerves and that she was probably late because she had a lot on her mind, with getting ready to leave and all.

"You're probably right," RC assured her.

Nicki didn't think about it anymore.

* * * * * *

On April 11, 1969, Nicki arrived at the American Airlines Stewardess College. There were lots of girls from all over the United States coming together to train. Out of six classes, there were only five black women. Nicki felt great to be one of those five chosen. In the beginning, the instructor taught about the planes, and locating the emergency equipment in case an emergency landing had to take place. Her roommates were from four different states. Nicki's hair was cut really short, and she learned how to apply make-up properly. They were also fitted for stewardess uniforms and choose shoes in colors of navy and red or plain navy. Nicki was having the time of her life. She and RC talked on the phone a lot.

After three weeks of training, however, Nicki still had not started her period. RC told Nicki it was up to her to decide what she wanted to do. By

My Mother's Black Child

that time, Nicki knew she was pregnant, and she had to make that choice real soon. She felt she couldn't have an abortion, so that left only one option, to have the baby. It was the hardest decision she ever had to make in her life. She informed her supervisor that she was resigning because she was getting married. That wasn't true, but she thought it was the best thing to say. The next day, Nicki packed and left for Illinois. RC met her at the O'Hare Airport in Chicago. They drove back to Rockford.

She stayed with her girlfriend, Doris, for a while and then she went to Arkansas to see Willie and her grandparents. They were all really glad to see her and Bo especially was happy to see her. He told her that he was married to girl named Emma Jean and they had three kids, two boys and a girl. Nicki told Bo that she was pregnant. Bo was anxious and excited to see the baby after it was born.

Chapter 5

Nicki left for Rockford the next day. She made an appointment to see the doctor. A few days later, tests were done. The doctor told her that she was pregnant, and that the baby was due in December. When she got home, RC was waiting to hear her confirm the news. "Ok," he said, "I think you should move in with Rose because I will pay her so you can stay there and maybe you can help her with her kids."

Rose had three children, two girls and a boy. They were good kids, so Nicki didn't mind doing that.

My Mother's Black Child

RC paid Rose and Nicki liked being around to help take care of the kids. She thought they were smart, and they liked her, too.

One thing bothered Nicki though, since she never heard from Reather. She knew Reather knew she was back. Birdie, her younger sister had seen her around town, so word had got back to Reather, Nicki was sure of that.

* * * * * *

Months passed and Nicki began to look forward to the birth of her own baby. She wondered if it would be a boy or a girl. RC wanted her to have a boy, but it didn't matter to Nicki, just as long as it was healthy. She also didn't have any names picked out, but felt that was Ok, because when the time came, she was confident she would think of something. An apartment of her own was something else Nicki wanted, and RC promised to buy new furniture for it. Shopping for baby clothes became a big past time and she always found herself looking at boy things.

On December 13, 1970, Nicki gave birth to a baby boy. She named him Cory. Actually, Birdie named him. He was a very cute baby and Nicki was a proud mother. RC sent Nicki flowers in the hospital and he was very happy that a boy had been born. Rose also visited Nicki while she was still in the hospital and expressed her joy for Nicki.

A few days later, Nicki was released from the hospital and went to stay with Rose until six weeks was up. Then, she moved into her own apartment. RC bought furniture for her, just like he promised he would, and Cory even had his own furniture. Coincidentally, Reather lived down the street from Nicki and she loved little Cory. Cory was medium brown skinned and not dark like Nicki. But Nicki didn't care what Reather liked or disliked.

Nicki's younger sisters, Birdie and Phyllis would baby-sit Cory a lot even if Nicki didn't need them. RC liked having the sisters around, but he didn't care too much for Reather. Nicki knew that the reason was because of how Reather felt about darker skinned people. He always said she was crazy, that he couldn't understand how a mother could feel that way about her own kids.

Finances were getting tight and Nicki made the decision to get on welfare. She didn't like it, but Cory needed a medical card and the Food Stamps helped. When Nicki told Reather she exclaimed, "I never had to get on welfare!"

Nicki retorted, "That's because you gave your kids away!" Reather didn't say anything else. The rift between mother and daughter forced Nicki to make a vow that she wouldn't be around Reather as much as she had in the past.

RC agreed with her, "I told you your mother is crazy!"

A few weeks later, Nicki moved to a different apartment. This one was better with all

My Mother's Black Child

new appliances and two bedrooms. Cory could have his own room and Nicki bought some more new furniture so he would have a bigger bed when he outgrew his crib.

* * * * * *

On November 13, 1971, Reather got a phone call from Arkansas, telling her Bo was dead. Reather couldn't believe it. He had been gambling with another man and that man had shot Bo several times in the back. Reather cried and screamed, "No! No! Not my son! Lord, not my son!"

The day after she got the news, Reather, and Kris, went down to Arkansas. Nicki, Birdie, and Phyllis left two days later. Alice didn't go at all.

Nicki felt so sorry for Emma Jean with three little kids to raise alone, but she also had a hard time dealing with the death of her brother. At least, those children were raised together, had the same father, and their birthdays were in the same month. Sadly, Nicki realized that Bo hadn't had the chance to meet Cory, something he wished for when they last spoke.

The day of the funeral was the saddest day of Nicki's life. She witnessed the coffin being carried out of the Hurse. It was raining, cold, and there stood her brother's three little children who didn't have a father anymore. Willie, Shorty, and Rutha, felt such sorrow because they had raised Bo. They went to the cemetery and as the coffin was

Necholia Johnson Beck

lowered into the ground, Nicki realized that this was real. He really was dead. She would never see him again. She started crying and couldn't stop. Shorty was crying, too. Aunt Boo had kissed Bo good-bye at the church. Nicki remembered touching Bo. He felt cold like a brick. She would never forget that feeling.

Later, everyone went back to Bo's house to be with Jean and the kids. Reather started blaming Rutha and Shorty for Bo's death. "You should have never let him go to places like that!" she ranted. "If you had raised him right, this would have never happened."

Nicki spoke up and told Reather, "You are wrong to blame them for Bo's death because he was a grown man. If anyone is to blame, then you are Reather, because after all, you should have raised him yourself. He was your son and Dad's, not grandpa and Aunt Boo's."

Reather didn't say anything else after that. She just started crying again.

The next day, everyone departed back for Rockford. Jean and the kids came to Rockford for a week. Then they left back for Arkansas. Nicki had a hard time dealing with Bo's' death for several months. She thought about him a lot and missed him. Reather didn't talk about him very much so Nicki felt lonely.

RC had begun seeing other women and didn't deny it. "Yes, I am and I'm sorry if you can't accept that."

My Mother's Black Child

It broke Nicki's heart but she couldn't continue seeing RC after that. She contacted a friend in California to find out if she could locate an apartment for Cory and herself. Lillie lived in Los Angeles. She found Nicki a nice apartment nearby. Then Nicki got a job as a sales clerk and Cory was put into daycare. Lillie loved Cory a lot. Since she couldn't have any children of her own, she was really crazy about him.

The two went out to bars and had a good time. Nicki thought about RC but it just wasn't the same. Lillie would keep Cory sometimes, just to have him around her. Reather never called Nicki and Nicki didn't call her. Birdie would send lots of letters and one even included her school picture.

RC sent Cory money for Christmas and he also called. But Nicki still didn't miss him. In February of the following year, she learned from a girlfriend in Rockford, RC had been arrested for drugs and was going to prison. She also was told he had gotten a divorce. Later, she would find out he got married to another girl and still went to prison.

California proved to be too fast for Nicki so she decided to move back to Rockford. Cory missed Lillie a lot after they left.

When she returned to Rockford, Nicki found a job, but moved into the Rockford Housing Authority Fairgrounds project complex. It was a two-bedroom apartment. They stayed for a long time and when RC got out of jail, he visited Cory. Cory didn't seem to remember him much, but at least he had a father in his life. That fall, Cory started the afternoon kindergarten class.

* * * * * *

A lot of years have come and gone since that time. Reather and Nicki still do not talk too much. Cory is nine years old now and Nicki is pregnant with her second child.

On November 13, 1980, the phone rings. It is one of Nicki's acquaintances, George. He blurts out, "Hello, Nicki, this is George. Turn on the TV. I think RC just got killed. It's on the news right now."

"When did this happen?"

"I think it happened last night in Chicago."

"Oh my God," Nicki exclaims, "I've got to tell Cory. Thanks for calling, George."

Nicki hung up and turned on the TV. The news wasn't giving many details regarding how it happened, but it did confirm names of the victims and RC was one of them. When she heard RC's name mentioned, Nicki called her sister Kris. They both went to pick Cory up from school so she could tell him what happened to his father. Cory cried and Nicki held him, telling him it would be all right.

Nicki didn't go to the funeral, but she did take Cory to the visitation. She didn't think she would be able to stand the memorial service, as she was six months pregnant. "I feel as though I lost my best friend," she confided to RC as she looked down at him in his coffin. "You were the only one who

My Mother's Black Child

knew me and helped me get over my feelings about the color of my skin. I'm going to miss you." Nicki stood, looking at RC, "I'm so very sorry this happened to you, so very sorry." Cory came up and looked at RC. He started crying. The feelings of sadness were so overwhelming they had to leave.

She kept thinking about RC all that night and the days and months to come. *He was my best friend, and I know I'll never find anyone else like that again in this life. I'm going to raise Cory not to get involved in drugs of any kind. I'm going to have this baby in a few months and I'll be glad.* Then the realization that RC had died on November 13th, the same day Bo had died, hit her. *This is the second person I loved to die on November 13th. It must be a bad number for me. I hope not, though.*

* * * * * *

On February 23, 1981, Nicki gave birth to a baby girl. Her name was Ericka, and she was pretty. She had darker skin than Cory, but that didn't matter to Nicki. She loved Ericka regardless. Cory was happy he had a little sister and helped Nicki wherever he could. Reather didn't say much about Ericka when she saw her, but again Nicki knew the reason why. Ericka wasn't a high yellow or light enough for her.

Five months later, in August, Nicki received a call from Willie. He said Shorty was missing and the police hadn't found him. Aunt Boo had a heart attack with the stress of it all, and she was in the hospital in Gurdon. Nicki responded, "Ok, Dad, I'm coming home."

"I'll see you when you get here," Willie said and then he hung up.

Then Nicki called the hospital where Rutha was admitted and talked to her nurse, "I hope she will be all right."

The nurse informed her that Rutha was resting well, "I'll call you if her condition changes. Please leave your phone number."

Later that same night, the nurse called back and told Nicki that her grandmother had passed away. Nicki started crying. "Thank you for calling."

Willie called a few minutes later, and Nicki told him, "I already know Dad, Aunt Boo is dead."

"That's right baby, and they haven't found Daddy yet. I don't know what I'm going to do now."

"Dad," Nicki assured him, "Don't worry. It will be all right. We will survive this."

Reather called the next day to tell Nicki she had heard the news. "I'll keep Cory and Ericka if you want me to," she stated.

Nicki countered, "I can't afford to take both of them on the plane with me. You can keep Cory, but I'm taking Ericka with me."

Reather agreed to do that, "Ok, I'll keep Cory." It always came back to the fact Reather treated people with dark skin different, worse, in fact because of the color of her skin. Baby or not, that was just how Reather felt, and Nicki couldn't

My Mother's Black Child

afford to take a chance that she would harm her baby.

She left the next day, taking Ericka with her. Nicki stayed with her Aunt Mattie and Uncle Ernest. Aunt Mattie was Willie's sister, so all of Nicki's cousins were there, too. Ericka cried the whole time they were down in Arkansas because of the heat. It was unbearable.

In order to relieve Ericka of the heat, Nicki called the funeral home and talked to the director. "Can I see Aunt Boo's body earlier because we have to leave earlier than planned?" she asked.

"I can arrange that," the funeral director answered, "But she won't be dressed."

"That's fine," Nicki said.

When Willie came over, Nicki told him, "The heat is making Ericka sick. I have to leave tomorrow."

Willie understood that not everyone could take this kind of heat.

Sammy, Nicki's cousin and his wife, took her to the funeral home to see Aunt Boo's body. Nicki cried and said, "She looks just like she's asleep." Afterward, Nicki said her good-byes and headed back to Rockford.

The next day, Reather brought Cory over. Ericka was fine now that she was out of that Arkansas heat. Tuesday, Willie called with the news that they had found Shorty's body in the woods near the house. His body was badly decomposed, so they would have to have a close-casket funeral. Nicki cried upon hearing that, "I'm so sorry, Dad, but at least we know now where he is."

"I guess you're right baby," Willie agreed. He hung up the phone and Nicki was left to think about Grandpa and Aunt Boo a lot that day.

* * * * * *

It is December 1, 1984, and Nicki has moved out of the projects. She lives in a nice neighborhood in a house on the East side of Rockford. Cory attends High School and Ericka is in grade school.

As part of the whole story, Nicki appeared on the Oprah show on May 12, 1987. The topic of the show was "Racial Prejudice Within the Same Race." Nicki talked about her relationship with her mother. There were other guests who appeared with similar experiences. Reather didn't like the fact Nicki went on national TV and told the whole country about the problems between them. For a long time, Reather and Nicki didn't talk to each other.

Cory graduated from Rockford East High School on June 3, 1988. Reather died on June 23, 1990 of lung cancer. The week of her death, she called Nicki to express her remorse, "Nicki, I am so sorry for what I did to you a long time ago and you are in my will just like the other kids."

My Mother's Black Child

Nicki was so shocked to hear that, she stated, "I've waited all my life to hear you say that. Now, I'll come to see you."

"You take care of yourself," Reather told her, "Make sure you take care of Cory and Ericka, too."

"Ok, I will," Nicki responded.

Both Nicki and Ericka went to Reather's funeral. There were a lot of people who paid their last respects. All of Nicki's sisters attended, and Birdie was the only one who was nice to her.

Ironically, three weeks later, Nicki found out that Reather did not have her in the will like she had said, but it was just like Reather to lie even on her deathbed.

Necholia Ann Johnson Beck was married four years and divorced. Nicki attended American Airlines Flight School, Dallas-Fort Worth, Texas, and Rockford Business College, Rockford, Illinois. She still lives in Rockford, Illinois, and is employed with the Rockford Public Schools. Both her children are grown now. Her son is married and lives in California. Her daughter lives in Illinois and has her own family.

Necholia Johnson Beck

AUTHOR'S SPECIAL NOTE

Willie Johnson Jr. died February 3, 1998, in Hope, Arkansas. He had been sick a long time with Alzheimer's. At the time of his death, Dad was 73 years old. He is buried in Gurdon, Arkansas.

Printed in the United States
22347LVS00001B/202-216